Made in Suede

This attractive two-colour knee-length coat is made from six skins

To. my Lady Mead?

Made in Suede
The Art of Tailoring in Soft Leather

BRENDA MILLS

Best Wishes.

Brenda.

LONDON: G. BELL AND SONS, LTD

ISBN 0 7135 1765 4

Printed in Great Britain by
The Camelot Press Ltd, London and Southampton

I wish to express my thanks and appreciation to the following for their help and encouragement in the preparation of this book

Mr. J. D. Swanson, Group General Manager of Gomshall and Associated Tanneries, Gomshall, Surrey

Eric Doltan

and Jane Coveney, my right arm, without whom this book would not have been written

A man's jacket combining suede fronts and back with hand-knitted sleeves and front rib. For this garment you would need two skins

Contents

Contents—continued

The Photographs

Preface

Since the time of stone age man, animal skins have been recognized as a perfect material for making warm and attractive clothing, but during the past few years leather has been rediscovered. The many advances in technical processing have made leather finer and more supple; and now it is easier than ever for the enthusiastic home dressmaker to make a fashionable garment, comparable in every way to those bought off the peg.

In this book I aim to cover basic tailoring instructions as well as specialized techniques for dealing with leather. The first section gives detailed information on the properties of suede and grain leather, material handling and tailoring techniques; the second section gives step-by-step instructions on the making of a range of suede and leather garments which would be a sound foundation for any fashion-conscious woman's wardrobe.

BRENDA MILLS

Part I

Properties, Material Handling
and Tailoring Techniques

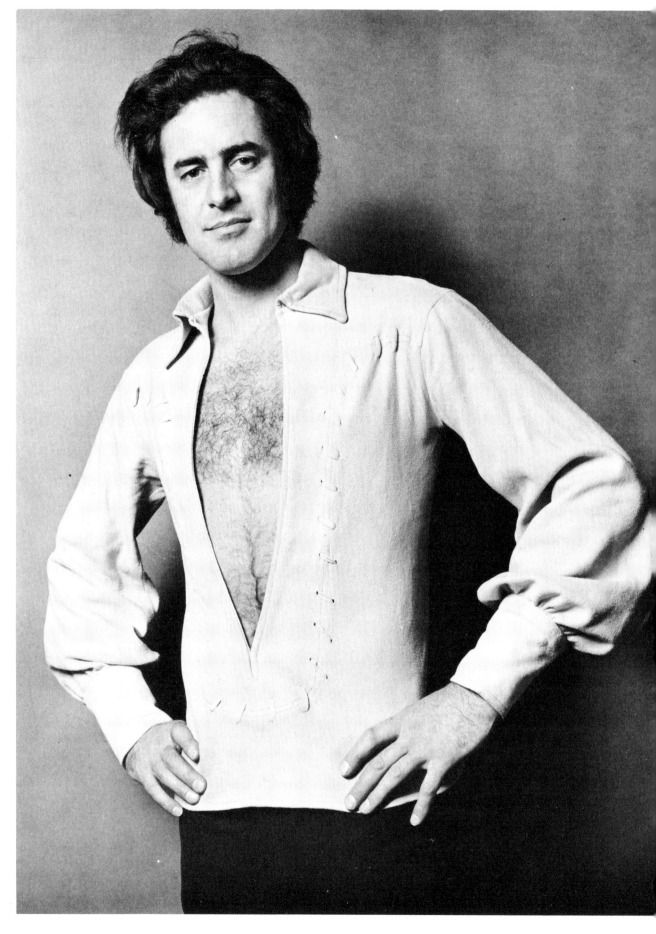

1. *What is Leather?*

Skins, unlike other clothing materials, are not of an even texture, having been part of a living animal. They have been chemically treated to produce a material of warmth, wearability and great attraction – leather.

Unfortunately for the dressmaker, animals do not come in uniform shapes or sizes and you must banish completely from your mind all preconceived ideas relating to any other materials with which you have worked. Having done this you must say to yourself, 'Here I have the skin of an animal which has lived and breathed and been subjected to processes of sun, wind, rain and cold.'

Areas (ii) and (iii) of Figure 1 are less hardwearing and should be avoided if possible when cutting, or placed in a less obvious position. Area (i) is not a weak part of the skin but it is less pleasing to the eye and because of its thicker construction cannot be matched against the remainder of the skin. It too should be avoided if possible.

In the main, clothing leathers are produced from sheep, calf, pig and goat skins. All of these are relatively small animals from which a limited surface area is obtainable. The size of the skins is also governed by the current public taste in meat. A joint now comes in popular 'Sunday' size, and so animals are killed when the carcass weight is correct. This, therefore, has an immediate effect on the size and thickness of the animal skin.

It would be inappropriate to deal with production, tanning and dyeing in detail in this book, but a brief outline of the tanning and dyeing processes is necessary to enable you to understand the nature of the material with which

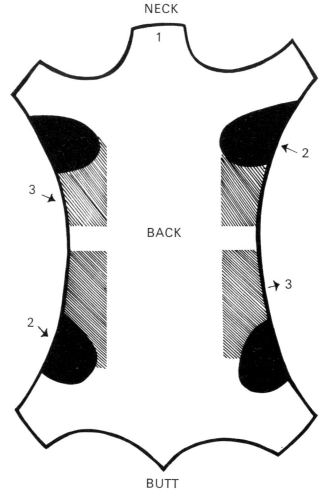

Fig. 1 The shape and properties of a typical sheep
pelt showing areas of differing texture

you are working. Tanning is the combining of the skin with certain chemicals
to produce leather which will not putrify and shrink as would happen to a
raw, untreated animal skin.

GRADING

Leather comes in grades denoting standards of quality. Thus Grade I skins
will be those in which the whole of the skin is of a good quality and from
which a large single perfect panel can be cut.

Grade II skins are those which have a slightly less perfect finish whilst Grade III skins will show more faults, most of which may be due to natural causes.

The skins in all grades will have been processed in the same manner and the differences in grading are largely due to the individual characteristics of the skin.

Warning

Take particular care when purchasing skins or skin garments abroad. In these times of modern travel many misguided souls return home from exotic holidays with bargain skins or garments, many of which contain pelts which have not been properly tanned. After a few months' wear they begin to putrify and any tick eggs lying dormant under the skin surface will hatch. This is particularly true of sheepskin coats and rugs purchased in the warmer climates.

I know of a particular instance where a sheepskin coat purchased in South America was taken to a tannery who were asked to investigate its extremely unpleasant odour. This was found to be due to incorrect tanning and as the rotting process could not be arrested the coat had to be destroyed.

The tanning process also determines to a large extent the properties of the leather, which can vary from a soft and supple product for gloves to a firm, hard finish for use by shoemakers as sole leather.

Dyeing is the process by which leather is coloured, using synthetic dye-stuffs. The choice of dyestuffs will determine the washability or amenity to dry cleaning, the fading properties and, of course, the colour of the leather. The skins are dyed in large quantities in drums, and a typical dye load can contain as many as 500 skins, although the exact figure depends upon available equipment and the process used. In the dyeing process a chemical reaction occurs between the tanned skins and the dye, and since none of the skins is identical, there can be slight differences in the chemical reaction of the skins which affect the amount of dye to which the skin will react. This leads to slight differences in shade which, despite all the efforts of the tanner, are unavoidable. *It is essential* to ensure that the skins purchased do match and that a sufficient quantity of skin is purchased to complete the garment, as it may not be possible to obtain additional matching skins at a later date.

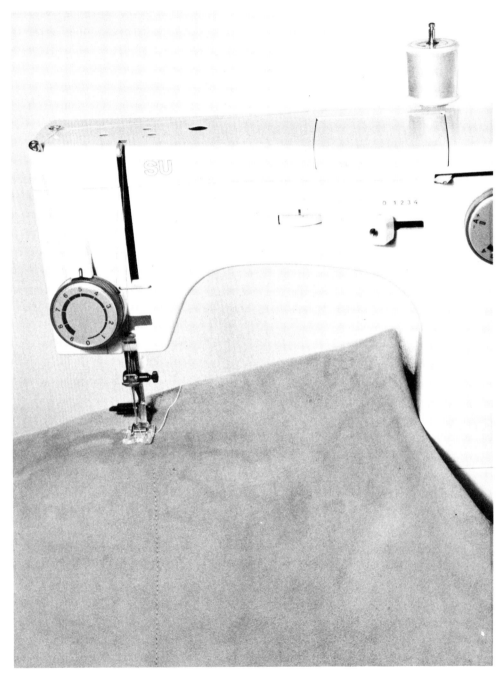

Sewing suede on a domestic sewing machine—note the size of the stitch

2. *Equipment*

Having the right equipment will make your tailoring work that much more professional. The most expensive equipment is not always the best, but it is certainly worthwhile investing in the little extras which will make your work more enjoyable.

BODKIN

The bodkin is used for removing tacking threads and is usually made from bone or plastic. It is blunt at the point and therefore will not damage the material.

DRESSFORM

A dressform is an extremely useful piece of equipment, especially for judging the set of the collar. One must curb the tendency to make the garment fit the model rather than the wearer! A great deal of practical knowledge of garment construction and fitting can be obtained by this means.

PINS

The most useful type of pin for suede or leather is the glass-topped type used in lampshade making. They are more expensive than ordinary plated pins but because of the fine points and the glass tops they puncture the skin without difficulty and are easier to push into place.

PUNCH PLIERS

Punch pliers are used to make the holes for thonging or for the eye of a tailor's hand-worked buttonhole. The six-way punch is the most useful, having six sizes on the same punch.

RULER

A 12-inch rule is used for measuring pockets, buttonholes, etc. It can be made in plastic, steel or wood. The type I prefer for tailoring in leather is the steel rule because it is more weighty and less likely to move in use.

SCISSORS

Eight-inch flat bottomed scissors are preferable when cutting leather, and long bladed scissors such as the type used for hairdressing are used when shearing wool from a shearling.

SEWING MACHINES

A sewing machine is only as good or bad as the user. Practice in all things makes perfect and this is especially so of sewing machines. Remember when working with leather to use the largest stitch on the machine except on the very fine suedes, and to release the pressure on the needle bar. This in turn controls the weight on the foot, which, if the pressure is heavy, will force the teeth underneath to cut into the skin.

Make sure that the machine is always clean and free from oil or grease. Be firm in the manner in which you feed the skin through the machine; do not pull the skin but help it feed through from the back.

SEWING NEEDLES

'Betweens' are the tailor's needles. No. 3 for heavy sewing and basting, through to No. 7 for finer work. They are all short needles and are less likely to bend or break in use.

Glover's Needles

Be very cautious of these. Having a diamond-shaped head they cut, and have a tendency to lift out small pieces of the skin.

Machine Needles

On the fine leathers such as many of the washable ranges a size 14 is suitable. As one goes through to the heavier suedes and leathers, 16s and 18s are used, 18s being the most suitable for sewing shearling.

TAPE MEASURE

A tape measure is made in linen, cotton or fibre glass. The cotton and linen ones do have a tendency to stretch and it is a good idea to check them against a yard stick from time to time.

THIMBLE

So many people say they cannot use a thimble. Rubbish! To sew efficiently with leather or with any other fabric a thimble is a must. Always remember to push the needle with the side of the thimble and not the top. I strongly discourage the use of plastic thimbles which are prone to split, and prefer the tailor's thimble which, having an open end, allows the finger to 'breathe'. This is important if one is sewing for long periods.

THREADS

I would never personally recommend the use of a synthetic thread with a natural fabric. The construction of the synthetic thread will not allow the machining to 'float' on top, which is very necessary when carrying out decorative stitching on leather or suede.

TRACING WHEEL

The tracing wheel is used for making imprints through cloth or paper on to paper underneath.

WASTE PAPER BASKET

A large waste paper basket is extremely handy as tidiness in the workroom is essential. Develop the habit of using the basket for waste and also keep a large carrier bag handy for scraps of leather which will undoubtedly be useful to you or your children.

3. Tailoring Terms

ARROWHEAD TACK (or *Spratsheads*)

Used for strengthening the ends of pleats. Mark a triangle at the bottom of the pleat with sides of half an inch and work as shown in Figure 2.

The needle enters the material first at the point then at the base until the triangle is covered. This is worked in buttonhole twist in a colour to tone with the skin.

BREAK

The break is the point where the turnings of the collar meet those of the front facing. The break finishes at the first buttonhole.

FACING

The facings should be cut down the straight of the skin. If possible each facing should be cut in one piece. In cloth tailoring a join is not acceptable in better class work; in leather tailoring it is acceptable. The join should be made on the cross (as a bias seam), excess should be trimmed away and the seam allowance secured with adhesive. Any thickness of skin can be minimized if the seam is hammered.

ARROWHEAD TACK

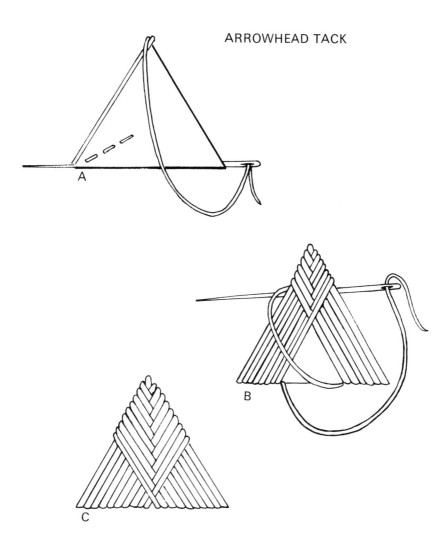

Fig. 2 Arrowhead tack as used for strengthening the ends of pleats, pockets, darts, etc.

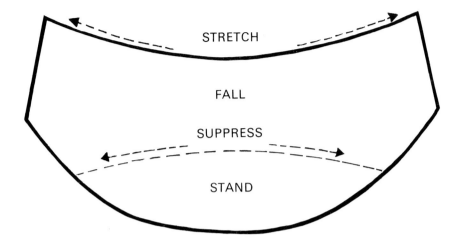

Fig. 3   Layout of a typical coat collar

FALL

This is the point of the collar that shows outside the neck of the garment as in Figure 3.

PADDING STITCH

Padding stitch is used on the collar of a garment and the lapels to hold the collar and the lapel in shape. This cannot be done with leather but the same effect can be achieved by holding the canvas firmly when securing to the facing with adhesive.

BASTING

The term used by tailors in place of 'tacking'. Basting is used to hold the garment in position prior to fitting or machining.

EASING

The method of reducing any fullness on sleeve-heads, bust, shoulder seams and elbows. In cloth tailoring 'easing' is achieved with the basting stitch and shrinking with steam. When tailoring in leather steam should not be used. The same result can be obtained by gently manipulating the skins by hand to lose any fullness.

4. *Adaptation of Patterns*

Exact stock size? Such people are few and far between; for most of us patterns need to be altered in some way to fit our individual requirements. The aim is to preserve the original fitting lines of the pieces, that is to say, the outside edges, and all alterations should be made inside these lines.

EXAMINING THE PATTERN

Sort the pattern pieces and compare them with the layout which accompanies them. Remember, leather is made up in a slightly different way. There will be printed instructions on various parts such as 'place to lengthwise fold' or 'place on the bias'. They do not strictly apply with leather (read cutting notes).

TURNING OR NO TURNING

Some patterns have turnings allowed and others are cut on the exact cutting lines. Make sure which type you have and if necessary allow $\frac{1}{2}$ inch or $\frac{5}{8}$ inch turning. Sewing lines are usually indicated by perforations or thick black lines. Always make turnings the same width or confusion may arise.

Methods of Adaptation

1: Remove your garment and arrange for someone to pin together the pattern on your figure; this can also be done before trying on. If you have a dress form adapted to your own measurements you can test the pattern on that.

2: Lay the pattern on a table, matching notches and with the edges touching if no turning allowed, or with turnings overlapping. The shoulders should be left open. With the tape measure apply your measurements in the position in which they were taken on the figure.

BODICE

When the back or the front of the garment bodice is too long: if the excess is below the neck and bust, or between the bust and the waist, or at both places, pin a tuck across whichever part applies: this will keep the underarm height in its proper place.

When the back or front of the garment bodice is too short: correct in the same place by cutting the pattern across and insert strips of paper as required.

When the back is too wide: is the excess width across the shoulder where the back measurement was taken or is it below the neck? For the former make a downward tuck slanting from the middle shoulder to the waistline, finishing about 2 inches from the centre back. This tuck can be graduated as required. If the fullness is below the neck only, insert pin tucks about $2\frac{1}{2}$ inches long.

When the back is too narrow: make a cut running down from the shoulder in a slanting direction to the centre back of the waistline. See Figure 3 (a). Separate the pieces and insert a strip of paper to the necessary width.

When the front is too wide: the excess width may be across either the chest and bust or just below the armhole, or at both places.

If excess is across the chest and bust, place a slanting tuck from the shoulder to the waistline; if the fullness forms at the front of the armhole, make a small dart running diagonally to the bust line, or make a small horizontal dart on the underarm edge about 2 inches down and paste on a small piece of paper to restore the armhole curve.

When the front is too narrow: if the front is in two pieces, separate and insert a strip to give the required width, then cut through the middle. Extra may be added to underarm if it is too narrow.

If the front is in one piece, cut down from the middle of the shoulder to the waist and insert a strip to required width as in Figure 3 (b).

BODICE ALTERATION—

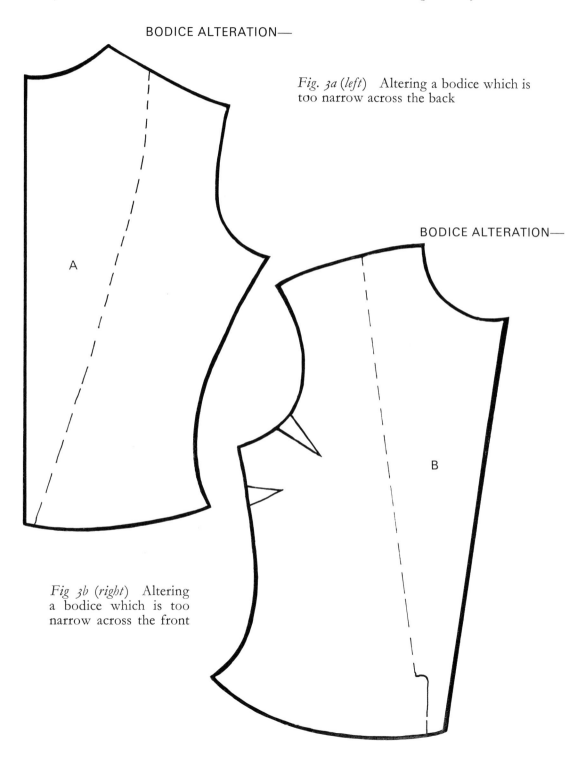

Fig. *3a (left)* Altering a bodice which is too narrow across the back

BODICE ALTERATION—

Fig 3b (right) Altering a bodice which is too narrow across the front

5. Patterns

SELECTING A PATTERN

Selection of the right pattern is most important when making a suede or leather garment, so study your build and decide which styles are most suitable for your figure type. You must bear in mind that suede and grain leather lend themselves more readily to a plain, tailored style and that gathers and tucks, etc., are most unsuitable for this type of material.

Begin by choosing a plain garment, because invariably the size of the skin is the deciding factor in the ultimate style.

Due to the size of the animal pelt it may be necessary to make joins, or a join across the back, forming a yoke. This line must be carried through on the front of the garment to give uniformity; such joins should be made into a feature of the garment by finishing either with saddle stitching on the edge, or edge stitching and $\frac{7}{8}$-inch stitching. This theme can also be carried out on pocket edges, collar revers and belts as in Figure 4. There are certain kinds of figures for which this type of join is more suitable than one across the hip. Figure type is most important, and a woman with a generous hip measurement would find a hip join most unattractive whereas a woman with an ample bosom would prefer a hip join, therefore giving a more balanced proportion to the garment.

The strongest part of the skin runs from below the neck to the tail, and it is also the most even in strength and texture.

It follows that the pieces of the garment requiring the most even part of the skin, for reasons of wear and appearance, should always be taken from the

Fig. 4 Garment showing top stitching, i.e. two rows of stitching $\frac{1}{8}$ inch and $\frac{5}{8}$ inch in, used as a decorative finish

centre back of the pelt. Foreparts (jacket and coat fronts) should both be cut from the same skin, as in Figure 5.

If you are unable to cut a complete back from one skin you must then decide at which point it is more desirable to place the join. Joins in the foreparts can be utilized for the pocket placing as in Figure 6.

Sleeves can be cut in one piece, or a top sleeve and an underside sleeve, or a sleeve with a seam through the centre as in Figure 7.

Repeat the top stitching to match the rest of the garment.

Very often it is possible to tip the pattern pieces to the left or to the right, thus obtaining the maximum use of available skins. One of the advantages of

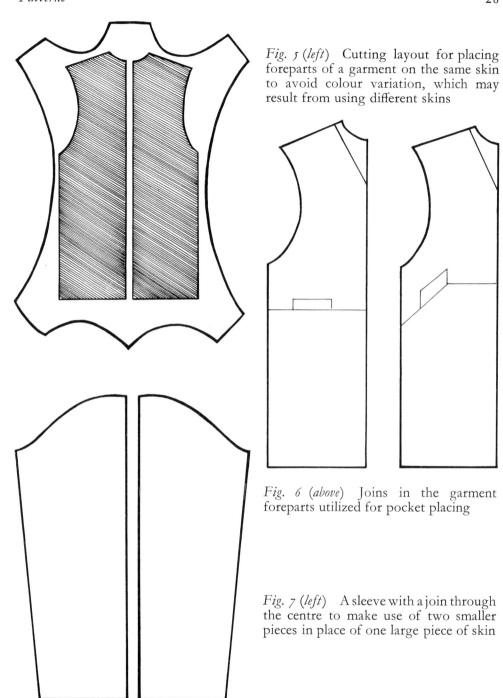

Fig. 5 (left) Cutting layout for placing foreparts of a garment on the same skin to avoid colour variation, which may result from using different skins

Fig. 6 (above) Joins in the garment foreparts utilized for pocket placing

Fig. 7 (left) A sleeve with a join through the centre to make use of two smaller pieces in place of one large piece of skin

working with skin is the absence of warp and weft. Always try to cut out sleeve heads from skins of a similar nature and texture as the armholes (or seye) of the garment. The reason for this is that if you use a thin loose skin for the sleevehead and a firmer skin for the armhole, the appearance of the sleevehead will become droopy as the one has not the strength to support the other. The part of the facing that has the turn for revers and the top collar should also be cut from an even piece of skin, and the parts of the skin that are not quite perfect can be used under the collar.

The front facing can also be joined as long as the join is below the top buttonhole and does not in any way interfere with subsequent buttonholes.

When placing your pattern pieces, work with the right side of the skin uppermost – this ensures that any flaws are visible and you can cut to avoid them. All pieces of the garment should be cut in a single layer, *NEVER* folded. Duplicate pattern pieces to be cut on the fold are those specified to be cut more than once. To duplicate a pattern to be cut on the fold, fold a piece of brown paper along the centre line. Chalk around the pattern and cut. Then open out the paper. You will now be able to trim along the chalk lines leaving a duplicate pattern piece. Single pieces such as sleeves and foreparts must be made in separate pieces making sure that a 'right' and a 'left' side are cut out. A mistake here could cause you to have two right sleeves or two left sleeves. With other materials one can always buy extra and make good the error, but with suede or leather this is not easy, a good match being difficult to obtain.

RULES OF CUTTING

It is essential to have a large smooth surface on which to cut, and to assemble all your required tools beforehand. Examine your paper pattern, which should have been adjusted to fit your personal measurements, as already described. Place the skins in sizes. For example, place all 7 ft skins, all 6 ft skins and all 5 ft skins together so that if you want to use your larger skins for the most important pattern parts first, you can more easily lay your hands on them. Plan out all parts of the pattern and do not be satisfied with your first attempt but juggle the pieces around with the firm aim in mind: to cut all the pattern pieces with as little wastage as possible. It is comparatively easy to cut out a garment from a large amount of skin, but often it seems impossible to cut your garment from the amount of skin you have at hand. So you must learn to treat your pattern as a jigsaw puzzle and your pieces will all fit. I personally find this part of the operation one of the most stimulating because it is indeed a challenge.

If you are satisfied that all the pieces have been accounted for and that 'left' and 'right' are correct (too much importance cannot be placed upon this operation) use weights or other heavy objects to hold the patterns in place on top of the skins, and take ordinary blackboard chalk (*not* tailor's chalk nor dust free chalk) and mark around the edges of the pattern. The chalk should be used on its long side, because if used in this manner it is easier to remove marks should any error have been made and no 'scouring lines' will be left on the suede nap.

Darts, buttonholes, hem lines, etc., should be marked at the same time. Place the chalk in the right hand and rub your thumb nail down the chalk to leave a small deposit of powder in the perforations on the pattern. If the pattern does not have perforations for seam allowance, etc., chalk round outside of pattern. Push pins through the dart markings, etc., and lift pattern carefully, leaving pins in an upright position, lightly sticking into the suede. Take ruler and chalk and mark along pin line.

After removing the pattern, join all the perforations together with a ruler and chalk. This is done only on one side of the garment: these marks are transferred on to the other side by placing the two pieces together, right side to right side (making sure that they are completely level) and applying pressure with the flat of the hand, using a striking method. The chalk marks having been transferred on to the piece below, separate the pieces; the lines will now be blurred so you must rechalk them slightly. This will ensure that the buttonholes, pockets or darts are level on each piece.

All darts should be cut through the centre; if the dart is left uncut it will cause an unsightly ridge where the sharp edge of the fold shows through on pressing.

Proceed to cut out the garment, taking long, clean and firm cuts, keeping the shears close to the table. (Short cuts would cause a jagged edge.)

PREPARE FOR FITTING

Use cellulose tape (Sellotape or Scotch Tape). Cut strips 2 to 3 inches long and stick by a small corner to the edge of the table.

Cut out 12 of these pieces at a time, the reason for this being that you will need your fingers to hold darts and seams together and it is practically impossible to cut the tape and hold seams together at the same time. With the right side of the garment flat on the working surface, hold the dart perforation together and tape across as in Figure 8. Use tape at intervals of $1\frac{1}{2}$ inches to 2 inches.

Having done this, tape the shoulders and the side seams together in the same manner and proceed to fit.

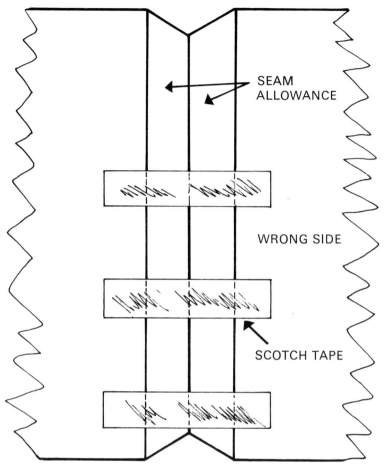

SEAM
ALLOWANCE

WRONG SIDE

SCOTCH TAPE

Fig. 8 Fitting preparation using Sellotape or Scotch Tape method

If the pattern has been adapted to your personal measurements as it should have been, any fitting requirements should be negligible. You must resist the temptation to keep trying on at every stage of its development as this is unnecessary.

Plan your fittings and stick to them. See that pockets and buttonholes are marked to suit the garment and the wearer's figure.

A seam held together with cellulose tape prior to fitting

6. The First Fitting

Place the garment very carefully on the figure and peg or paper clip the front so that the centre front marks come on top of each other; this is important. Make sure that the garment has been put on correctly, and then attend to the faults in the following order:

SLEEVE FITTING FAULTS

If the sleeve appears too long or too short this can be corrected by using clothes pegs or paper clips to hold up turnings.

If the sleeve appears too wide you can pin the sleeve back the amount to be reduced.

If the sleeve is too narrow make a note to let out the required amount.

COAT FITTING FAULTS

The coat should rest easily on the figure. Do not fit too closely and if the garment is small across any point remove the adhesive tape from the seam $\frac{1}{2}$ inch at a time. Peg or paper clip together in the required position. Check the position of the pockets.

Collar fitting faults are attended to at the next fitting.

With the absence of tacking it is useful to use paper clips to hold together the seams prior to machining. All darts are machined from the wide part towards the narrow part. With other materials one would usually machine

½ inch from the bottom of the dart, but to ensure a smooth bubble-free dart it is advisable to machine to the bottom of the dart making sure that the angle of machining is as in Figure 9.

Any tendency to finish too quickly causes a bubble at the bottom of the dart as shown in Figure 10.

Proceed to cut down the width of the dart and apply a thin smear of suitable adhesive such as Copydex to hold the dart open along both sides.

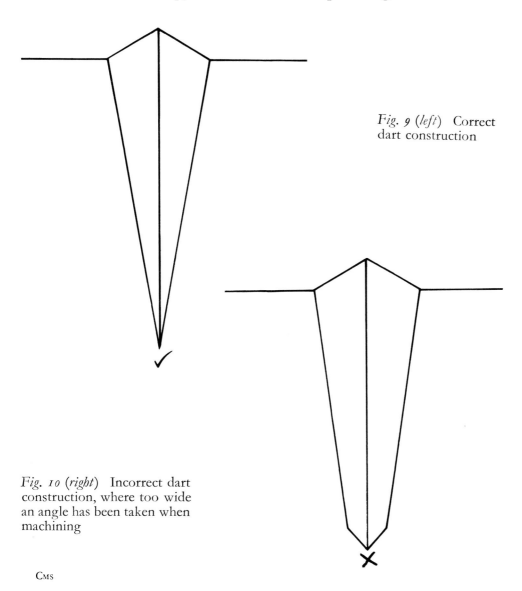

Fig. 9 (left) Correct dart construction

Fig. 10 (right) Incorrect dart construction, where too wide an angle has been taken when machining

7. Pockets

PATCH POCKETS

Patch pockets are made in many shapes, sizes and types according to the garment, but the construction is basically the same. The pocket has canvas on the wrong side to give a crisp appearance and to hold the pocket in shape. A patch pocket is always lined and has $1\frac{1}{2}$-inch facing, which is left on if possible when cutting.

Construction

1: Cut two pockets, one right and one left.
2: Cut two pocket linings slightly smaller than the pocket itself.
3: Cut two pieces of canvas $1\frac{1}{2}$ inches smaller across the top and $\frac{1}{2}$ inch smaller at both sides and at the bottom than the pocket.
4: Iron on the canvas and cut in $\frac{1}{2}$ inch each side of the pocket top. Proceed to turn in the edges $\frac{1}{2}$ inch on both sides and on the bottom edge.
5: Machine the lining on to the facing and then turn the facing to the edges and secure them with a smear of adhesive. Baste the lining on to the patch $\frac{1}{8}$ inch from the edge and then fell or hem into place.
Remove the basting thread and press with an iron on medium heat.

Placing Pockets

To secure on to the forepart make sure that the pockets are clearly marked. Place a small spot of adhesive on to each corner of the patch (on the wrong side) and place on the forepart of the garment. Machine on pocket, using edge stitching $\frac{1}{8}$ inch in.

A variation can be added by placing a second row of stitching $\frac{5}{8}$ inch in to give a heavier effect.

The stitching on the coat edges, collar, or any other part should follow the same theme.

THE POCKET FLAP

This type of flap is usual on the more casual type of garment to hide the mouth of a much used pocket.

The style of the flap must match the general style of the garment, that is, a square front must have a square flap and a rounded coat front should have a rounded flap.

The edge of the flap must follow the contour of the coat. The flaps should be designed and cut accurately at the fitting stage.

Construction

1: Draw the finished size and shape of flap so that you can see how it will appear on the finished garment.
2: Cut two flaps, one right and one left, two linings the same size and two pieces of canvas $\frac{1}{2}$ inch smaller than the pocket flap.
3: Iron the canvas on to the wrong side of the pocket flap and turn in the edge $\frac{1}{2}$ inch on the sides and at the bottom. This is done with a thin smear of adhesive.

   Hammer the edges to lay them flat, paying particular attention to any thickness at the corners. Ensure that the edge stitching on the flap matches any other top stitching. Lay the lining $\frac{1}{8}$ inch inside the outer edges and baste and fell into position.

Points to Watch

1: Ensure that all edges are straight and curves are regular.
2: Both flaps must be a matching pair and if curved must be curved at the same angle.
3: If cornered, they must be absolutely square.

THE WELT POCKET

This type of pocket is undoubtedly the strongest pocket for hard wear. The welt pocket can be made vertical, slanting or fancy.

Cut two pocket welts, if slanting, one right and one left. The size of the welt is taken from the width of the hand across from the base of the thumb to the base of the little finger plus $\frac{3}{4}$ inch at each end. This ensures that the hand will fit into the pocket with reasonable comfort.

Cut the pocket welt as in Figure 11; fold along and nip in $\frac{3}{4}$ inch from the ends of the crease, then slice away the corner triangle.

Cut the interfacing and iron into place on the top part of the pocket welt as in Figure 12; trim away the interfacing $\frac{3}{4}$ inch away from the welt sides.

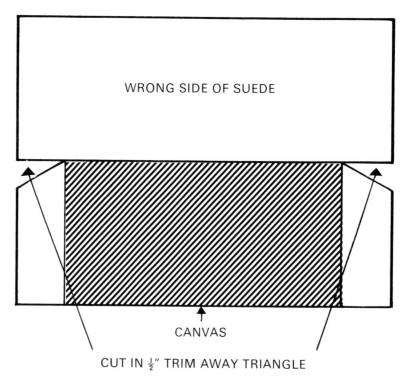

WRONG SIDE OF SUEDE

CANVAS

CUT IN $\frac{1}{2}$" TRIM AWAY TRIANGLE

Fig. 11   Pocket welt

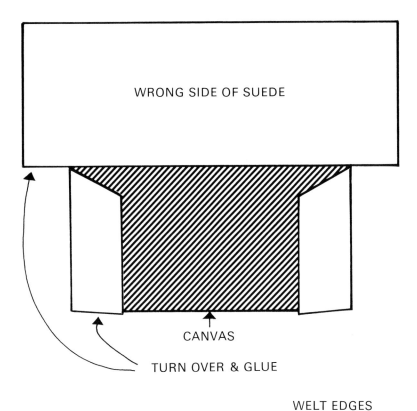

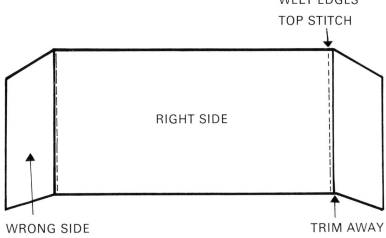

Fig. 12 Pocket welt construction

8. Underpressing

Underpressing is the pressing of all seams and darts prior to the assembly of the garment.

As each piece is machined it is opened by running the thumb through the middle of the seam. Then a light smear of adhesive is applied to the turnings, after which the seam is pressed on the wrong side.

Never force steam into suede or grain leather – the iron should be used dry at all times. Never use cloth or the 'lint' will be left on the suede or grain leather surface, leaving behind a slight 'fuzz' which is extremely difficult to remove.

Brown paper fortunately has no ill effect upon the skin so this can be used as a pressing cloth. I find that as long as the iron is not left on the skin, but kept moving, and the suede nap is brushed up with a soft, clean clothes brush afterwards, this is all that is needed to achieve a professional finish.

9. Top Pressing

This is done prior to the lining being put in. If the top pressing is left until the garment is completely finished, it can damage the lining. All pressing is done on a thick pad on the sleeve board. The garment is pressed on the right side starting from the left forepart, front edge or hem. As each area is pressed, lay it straight on the board beyond the sleeve board.

10. Lining

CUTTING THE LININGS

Lining patterns must be taken from the parts of the actual garment and not from the paper pattern. All the side seams, shoulder seams and the centre back must be marked from the skin on to the lining.

Cut the lining $\frac{1}{2}$ inch longer than the hem line. Each part should be cut accurately and the $\frac{1}{2}$ inch left below the hem on each portion of the lining to allow for possible alteration during fittings.

MARKING AND PRESSING LININGS

Check that any alterations made to the garment have been made to the lining. When this is done, baste the seams together and machine, taking the same seam allowance as that taken on the garment.

PRESSING LININGS

Lining seams should never be pressed open, but always pressed flat towards the back of the garment on the wrong side, the padded side of the sleeve board being used. After pressing, handle carefully and there should be no need for further pressing of the garment at any stage.

RE-MARKING

Position on seam pockets, etc., after trying on the garment.

1 : Re-mark the seams and any other affected parts.
2 : Shape the front edge if necessary.
3 : Check and re-mark the pocket positions if necessary.

11. Buttonholes

THE JETTED BUTTONHOLE

The jetted buttonhole is the most suitable type for grain leather garments. The buttonholes are cut on the foreparts and the jetting of the buttonhole is sewn to the leather, cut and turned out, and the facing is put on to the back of the hole which is then finished.

Great care must be taken to mark the buttonholes the correct distance from the edges so that they will be in the correct position when the front edge of the garment is made up.

Construction

1: Mark the hole and cut the jetting to size.
2: Mark the buttonhole on the jetting and machine along each side taking a bare $\frac{1}{4}$-inch seam.
3: Secure by double stitching on the corners but do not machine across the ends.
4: Cut the jetting through, making a mitre on the corners as shown in Figure 13.

It is essential that the corners should be cut to the stitch and not through it. Turn out the jettings and use adhesive in the usual manner as in Figure 14.

Making sure they meet in the centre, place the forepart the wrong side down, lift up the edge and machine mitres across securely. Stick the jettings to the foreparts. Trim away any excess.

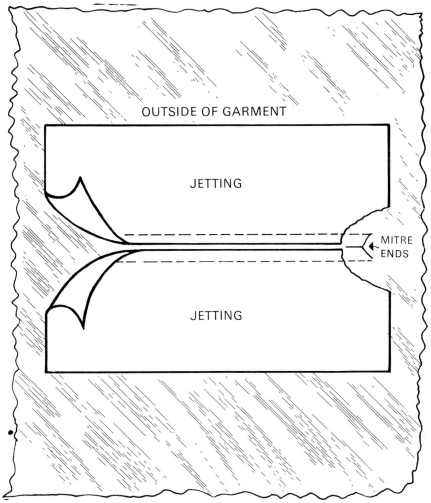

Fig. 13   A jetted buttonhole

THE TAILORED BUTTONHOLE

Tailors' buttonholes are worked with buttonhole twist and strengthened with a thick thread called 'gimp'. Practise well before attempting to do this on an actual garment. A sample should be made on a piece of double skin with a piece of canvas between.

Lay the button on the garment so that it rests $\frac{1}{4}$ inch from the edge. Sprinkle chalk through the buttonholes to mark the position of the button neck. Then move the button back so that it is just covering the chalk dots and mark the length of the hole, which should be slightly larger than the button.

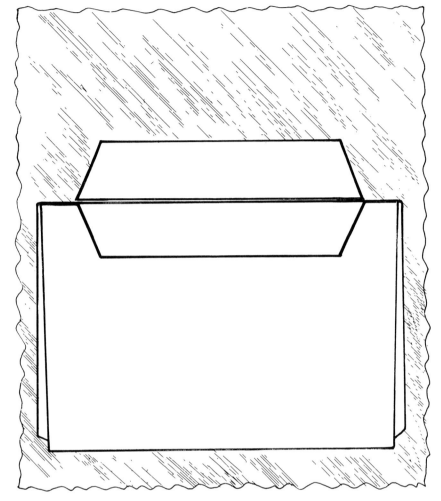

Fig. 14   Jetted buttonhole turned through after machining, and glued open

Tailored buttonholes have a tiny hole cut out of the end where the button rests when the garment is buttoned down. The hole is cut out with a buttonhole punch or a leather punch.

Construction

1 : Cut the hole starting at the eye, pierce the cloth with a sharp scissor and cut straight. Proceed to work buttonhole.
2 : Insert the gimp and hold it in position with the thumb. It should lie flat on the cloth at the other end. Stitch from the purl as shown in Figure 15.

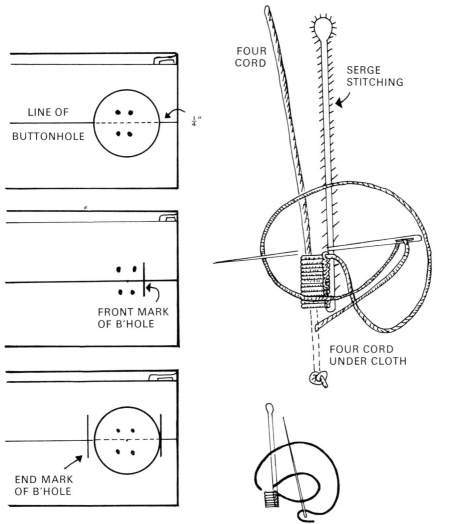

LINE OF
BUTTONHOLE

¼"

FRONT MARK
OF B'HOLE

END MARK
OF B'HOLE

FOUR
CORD

SERGE
STITCHING

FOUR CORD
UNDER CLOTH

Fig. 15   Tailored buttonhole worked with buttonhole twist and tailor's gimp

When working, the straight purl is pulled so as to lie flat between the two rows of stitches. When working the eye the stitch is pulled up to make a round hole for the gimp to be pulled through. The buttonhole is finished at the end with a bar. The bar is made by taking three stitches across and working them with a loop stitch. Before making the bar, the gimp is passed under the cloth and drawn lightly before cutting off.

Points to Aim at

1: All stitches must be the same length and evenly placed.
2: An evenly round eye.
3: Do not pull the purl knot tightly but ensure the knot is looped.
4: Take a good hold to ensure that there is no chance of pulling away, but always aim at as narrow a stitch as possible.

This type of buttonhole is suitable for the softer types of suede and gives a tailored, professional look to suede garments. Even in these days of machinery a well-made hand buttonhole is a joy to behold and greatly adds to the look of the garment.

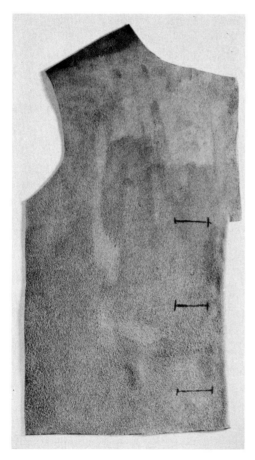 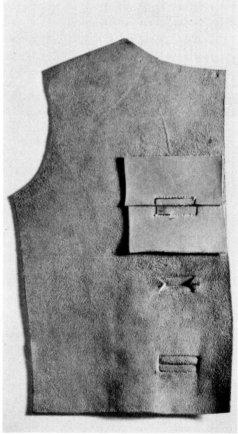

Marking foreparts for bound buttonholes

A jetted buttonhole in various stages of construction

12. Buttons

Buttons can help to make or mar a garment. A cheap button can ruin the appearance of an otherwise well-tailored garment, so do not skimp on buttons.

Always bear in mind that the surface of suede is matt and therefore to put on a shiny plastic button would be wrong. A good bone or suede-covered button is much more suitable, but remember that suede against suede always grips, so when making buttonholes which will be used against suede allow a little extra room.

Buttons can be made at a very reasonable cost but it is helpful to the manufacturer if you can give him thin pliable pieces of suede or leather. Such pieces lend themselves more readily to button machinery and moulds.

It is a good idea to have two extra buttons made as spares, as it is not always possible to have these made at a later date.

Buttons are purchased in sizes known as 'lynes': Ladies coat buttons, 40–45 lynes; Jacket buttons, 30–36 lynes; Cuff buttons, 22 lynes.

PUTTING ON BUTTONS

Place the garment on the figure and mark on the front edge position with chalk. Lay the garment flat on a table with the edges level at hem.

Scrape the chalk dust through the eye of the buttonhole with the thumb nail. Mark with a cross and sew button to centre of cross, using matching small buttons sewn underneath and leaving a neck in between the garment and the top button.

Take about four stitches through each hole in the button; strengthen this by winding the thread around and drawing tightly to form a neck.

13. *General Assembly Procedure*

Having completed all pockets, darts and in some cases buttonholes, you now proceed to machine together the garment.

If the lining has a centre back seam, machine together and press open. Machine any lining darts and press towards the centre back. Machine lining to facings and press towards the centre back.

Machine side seams and shoulder seams. Press.

Join top collar to lining at the centre back neck; finish machining at collar step. Make a cut on the collar at the shoulder seam and press open the seam from shoulder to step. The back neck seam is laid together.

If the skin is of a loose stretchy nature it is more satisfactory to machine $\frac{3}{4}$ inch wide tape to the seam.

Press with an iron on the wrong side of the garment to lay the seams flat. Proceed to machine on the under collar. Please note that the under collar is not canvassed.

Fold the collar in half and mark the centre on outside and inside edge. Fix with paper clips, starting at the back neck edge of the collar. The under-collar must be held firm, especially from the shoulder to the centre front.

Clip the undercollar to the curve if necessary, then open the seams and secure with a suitable adhesive in the usual manner.

At this point we move completely away from cloth tailoring. Turn in front edges $\frac{1}{2}$ inch from the top button to the hem, securing with adhesive, and hammer edges slightly to reduce any thickness. Having made sure of required length of garment, mark and turn a hem, securing with adhesive.

A dart cut through centre
from base to apex

A dart machined and
secured with adhesive

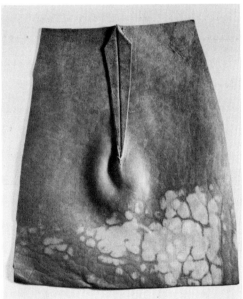

A hem being secured
with adhesive

Press on the wrong side with an iron at medium heat.

Baste in sleeves and machine with armhole edge on top, placing fingers of the left hand in between right side of armhole and right side of sleeve. Remove basting thread stitches and press seam towards sleeve hem. Tack armhole lining to sleeve and armhole, pull sleeve lining to sleeve head and pull to armhole covering previous stitches. Fell lining to coat hem. If loose lining is required, baste and turn up hem in appropriate manner. Press coat edges and collar, mark and stitch on buttons. Remove handling marks.

This is the general procedure for assembling a tailored garment.

14. Construction of a Simple Garment

A SUEDE SKIRT AND SLEEVELESS WAISTCOAT

As we have now covered the basics of suede and leather tailoring, we can proceed to the making of a suede skirt and sleeveless waistcoat, which should present no problems at all. Adjust the pattern if necessary to your basic measurements.

It should be possible to cut each garment out of two skins, making a total of four skins in all. Check these for any flaws and irregularities. Having noted them, lay the pattern pieces on to the skins. If all is satisfactory cut out the garment and tape the seams and darts together and fit. Make any alterations that are necessary and transfer these on to the skirt lining. Machine the skirt darts and press them open with your thumb. Smear with a light film of adhesive, lay them flat and press the darts with the iron on medium heat, using brown paper. Hammer away any thickness, especially at the apex of the dart. Machine the left-hand side seam. Commence machining $8\frac{1}{2}$ inches from the waist. Press open the seam and secure with adhesive in the usual manner, then continue to glue the seam flat to the top of the waistband as in Figure 16. The reason for this is that the seam will then lie flat, making it easier to insert the zip.

Glue zip on to the wrong side of the garment. Place the zip on seam allowance. Secure with a row of machining. Press the seam on the wrong side from the waistband to the hem.

With the work on the wrong side, machine the right-hand seam from waist to hem, which will have been held with paper clips on the wrong side.

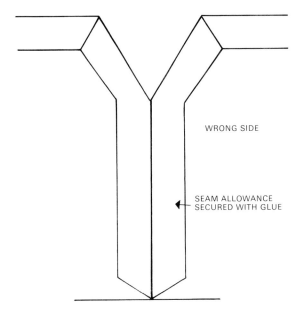

WRONG SIDE

SEAM ALLOWANCE
SECURED WITH GLUE

Fig. 16 Preparing for zip insertion with seam allowance secured with adhesive

Remove clips. Press the seam on the wrong side, securing lightly with adhesive. Peg the hem into the required position and fit.

The fit being correct, use adhesive to stick the hem into place, but do not be over-zealous with the glue – remember *A LITTLE GOES A LONG WAY*. If the hem has to be altered it is much easier to take down a hem that has not been too enthusiastically glued.

Press with an iron, on the right side.

The next step is to insert the lining. Place the wrong side of the skirt to the wrong side of the lining and check to ensure that the skirt lining is shorter than the suede garment. Hold the lining to the skirt waist with paper clips and machine the two together, taking $\frac{1}{4}$ inch turn in from the waist edge. Alternatively, use zigzag stitch to join the lining and the skirt together on waist edges.

THE WAISTBAND

Cut the waistband 3 inches wide and your waist length plus 2 inches: a 26-inch waist, for example, would require a 28-inch band.

Stiffen with Moyceel or petersham. Cut a strip 1 inch wide, the length of the skirt band. Chalk through the centre of the waistband on the wrong side, and then, if using petersham, secure the stiffening to the waistband with adhesive. Iron on if you are using Moyceel. (See Figure 17.) Machine the stiffening to the belt $\frac{1}{4}$ inch from the bottom of the stiffening on the wrong side, then press. The belt is now ready to be machined to the garment.

Mark the waistband to the required waist length leaving 1 inch at each end for fastening. The top piece of the waistband, without stiffening, is now machined on to the skirt waist, ensuring that the width above is equal to the width of stiffening. See Figure 18.

Press the seam towards the top of the waist, turn the petersham over on the inside as in Figure 19 and press with medium iron. Secure with adhesive.

Turn in belt edges as in Figure 20. Secure with adhesive and press with a medium iron and brown paper.

Stitch the waistband seam from the right side of the garment, going right into the seam that has been turned towards the top edge. If the seams have been placed in this manner, machining will automatically fall into position.

Fell the lining on to the back of the zip, ensuring that it does not interfere with the zip teeth, and work the buttonhole, press stud or belt clip to finish the waistband.

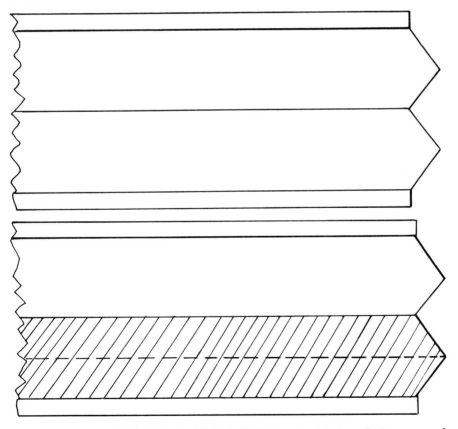

Figs. 17 and 18 (above) Waistband. *(Below)* Waistband with interfacing secured

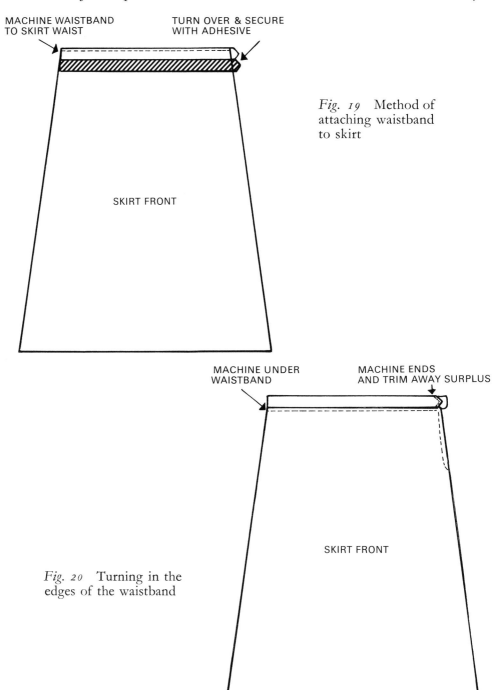

MACHINE WAISTBAND
TO SKIRT WAIST

TURN OVER & SECURE
WITH ADHESIVE

SKIRT FRONT

Fig. 19 Method of
attaching waistband
to skirt

MACHINE UNDER
WAISTBAND

MACHINE ENDS
AND TRIM AWAY SURPLUS

SKIRT FRONT

Fig. 20 Turning in the
edges of the waistband

Secure the lining hem at the side seams with french tack. To do this take a double thread and make three stitches from the lining hem to the skirt hem leaving $\frac{1}{2}$ inch thread between; hold taut and work into loop stitch as in Figure 21.

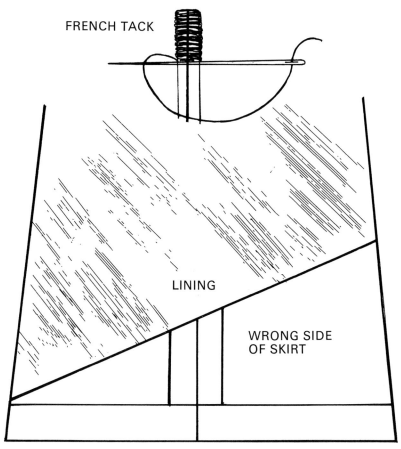

FRENCH TACK

LINING

WRONG SIDE OF SKIRT

Fig. 21   French tack, the method of attaching the lining to the skirt hem

Lightly press the hem and any other parts needing similar attention. Finally, lightly brush up the nap to eliminate any handling marks.

WAISTCOAT

Machine the lining, taking the same seam allowance as on the garment, press the seams towards the back and place on a coat hanger until needed.

Machine the waistcoat darts that have been held together with paper clips and press open the dart seams. Trim away any excess.

Press open with thumb and secure with adhesive. Press on the wrong side with a medium iron and brown paper. Fit the waistcoat, using paper clips to hold together side seams and shoulders. Turn up the hem of the garment with clothes pegs. Mark with chalk any alterations of turning on neck edges and armholes. If making buttonholes and pockets mark in their position at this stage.

Dismantle and make pockets and buttonholes as required. Press on the wrong side.

Chalk the finished hem line, machine together shoulder seams and side seams. Open with thumb and secure with adhesive. Press the garment on the right side with brown paper using a medium iron. Turn up the hem holding in place with pegs and glue sparingly.

Press on the right side with a medium iron.

Make $\frac{1}{4}$ inch turning around the front edge from hem to shoulder, shoulder to back neck, neck to shoulder and from shoulder to hem. This should be smeared with adhesive to secure.

Do not stretch on the straight edge or curve from bust to shoulder. Stretch a little around the back neck. If the suede is a little stubborn and will not give, stretch the amount required and, to make it sit comfortably, make tiny cuts to allow the curve to ease.

Press the edge with an iron and hammer any thickness that may result on the shoulder seams. If the skin is thick at that particular part, trim the corners of the seams away.

FACING NOTES

Cut the lining and cut the facing in suede if buttonholes are being made. If buttonholes are not required but other forms of fastening, it is quite adequate to make the lining exactly the same as the front of the garment, and fell the lining to the edge of the garment.

Machine the suede facing on to the lining on the foreparts. Machine back neck facing on to lining. Clip the lining in on the curve if necessary. To make sure the back neck is machined on evenly, mark the centre back of the lining.

Join together the lining, taking the same turnings as on the garment, and press the seams towards the back. The lining hem can be made loose or attached to the bottom of the garment with felling stitches. Mark and tack the lining, making sure that it will finish up $\frac{1}{2}$ inch shorter than the finished length of the garment. Fell the hem into place and remove the bastings. Press

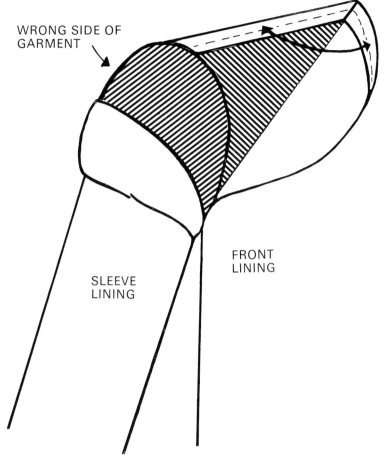

WRONG SIDE OF
GARMENT

FRONT
LINING

SLEEVE
LINING

Fig. 22   Attaching lining to shoulder

the hem, smooth any wrinkles in the lining and place on a coat hanger until required.

Mark the back neck at centre of both lining and waistcoat. Place the lining and the waistcoat together, wrong side to wrong side. Laying the shoulder seams together as in Figure 22, attach the lining to the shoulder seams, leaving 1 inch free at the neck edge and $\frac{1}{2}$ inch on the shoulder edge. Turn back the lining to the right side so that the lining is attached to the waistcoat on the shoulder seams. Check that it is hanging correctly, turn the back lining over again and secure the side seams to the side seams of the coat in the same manner, leaving 1 inch loose at the underarm edge and 1 inch loose at the hem.

This allows freedom to turn in lining at the sleeve edge. It may seem time-consuming but it is well worthwhile as it will do the very necessary job required of a lining, that is, to keep the garment in shape. Baste the lining to the armhole edge $\frac{1}{8}$ inch inside the fold edge of the waistcoat armhole. Do the same with the lining across the back of the neck and down the front edges. Fell into position and remove the bastings carefully. Rough treatment can result in the lining being disfigured.

Lightly press on the right side and brush up the nap to restore the suede surface. If the lining has a suede facing, glue the facing on to the foreparts and at the neck.

Commence work at the centre back and proceed to the hem on each forepart. The outside raw edge of the facing should protrude $\frac{3}{4}$ inch from the coat edge, which is then top stitched $\frac{1}{8}$ inch in, and the raw edge of the facing trimmed away, using scissors at a slanting angle.

Part 2

A Basic Suede and Leather Wardrobe

A lady's cardigan jacket combining suede fronts with knitted sleeves and back. This garment can be made from only one suede skin. It is suggested that a washable suede with the new 'superwash' hand knitting wool is used

15. A Suede/Wool Cardigan Suit

The traditional cardigan suit is a very versatile addition to any well-dressed woman's wardrobe. The English climate is so unpredictable that a warm lightweight garment is useful through any season. This suit can be made to combine knitting and suede, using suede for the skirt and the front panels of the cardigan. The skirt should be made in washable suede following the step-by-step instructions given in previous chapters. The knitting instructions can be used for a man's or woman's cardigan, reversing the buttons on the cardigan front.

Cut the suede to the required size, using Figure 23 as a guide. If a ribbed front is required omit the buttonholes on the suede front. Mark pockets and construct. Knitted ribs can be used following the welt method.

Cut a lining for the front of the garment but not for the sleeves or back as these are left unlined.

Join underarm seam on sleeve and press. Place knitted back on a soft pad or board. Fasten down with straight pins. Press with a damp cloth. Join knitted back to suede front at shoulders and side seams. Tack knitted sleeves into armholes and machine together, armhole on top.

If a knitted rib is required, centre the back neck of the garment and the centre of the rib by folding in half on the length. Tack rib on to garment, giving a little stretch from the shoulder to the first buttonhole. If the rib is left 'easy' in this area the garment will stand away from the chest.

If a knitted rib is omitted, turn over the suede front edges and secure with adhesive. This also applies to the hem of the suede front, which is stuck down when the side seams have been machined.

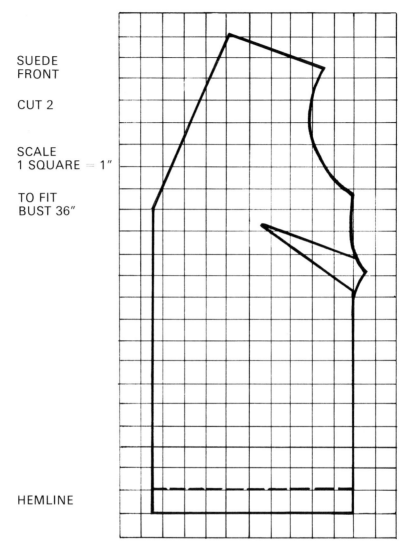

SUEDE
FRONT

CUT 2

SCALE
1 SQUARE = 1″

TO FIT
BUST 36″

HEMLINE

Fig. 23   Suede fronts cut to scale for knit/suede jacket

Tack the lining on to the rib and machine from the hem to the shoulders. Turn the lining over towards the side seams and stitch to the shoulders, front armhole edge and side seams. Stitch on buttons.

Press front of cardigan and brush to restore the suede nap.

CARDIGAN

Materials	16 (17) (18) (19) (20) ozs of Double Knitting Wool.
	2 No. 9 and 2 No. 11 knitting needles.
Measurements	To fit 34 (36–38–40–42 inch) bust or chest.
	Length (to back neck), 22½ (23¼–24–24¾–25½ inches).
	Sleeve seam 17 (17½–18–18½–19 inches).
Tension	6 sts. to 1 inch over pattern on No. 9 needles.
Abbreviations	

beg.	beginning
cont.	continue
dec.	decrease
fin.	finishing
foll.	following
g. st.	garter stitch
ins.	inches
inc.	increase
k.	knit
m.	make
m. st.	moss stitch
p.	purl
patt.	pattern
rep.	repeat
p.s.s.o.	pass slipped stitch over
rem.	remain
sl.	slip
sts.	stitches
st. st.	stocking stitch
tog.	together
wl. bk.	wool back
wl. fwd	wool forward
k. 1 below	k. into loop below next st.
Tw. 2	putting needles in front of last st., k. into front of 2nd st. then k. 1st st. and slip both sts. off tog.

BACK

With No. 11 needles cast on 106 (109–112–115–118) sts.

1st Row	P. 1 (tw. 2, p. 1) to end
2nd Row	K. 1 (p. 2, k. 1 below) to last three sts., p. 2, k. 1.

These two rows form the pattern and are repeated throughout. Continue straight for 3 inches then change to No. 9 needles and cont. straight until work measures 12½ (13–13½–14–14½) inches from beg., fin. with a wrong side row.

Shape Armholes	Cast off 3 sts. at beg. of next two rows.
Next Row	K. 2 tog., patt. to last 2 sts. k. 2 tog. t.b. 1.
Next Row	Pattern to end.

Repeat the last two rows five times more. 88 (91–94–97–100) sts. Continue straight until armhole measures 9 (9¼–9½–9¾–10) ins. fin.

SHAPE SHOULDERS AND BACK NECK

Cast off 6 sts. at beg. of next 4 rows.

Next Row	Cast off 6, patt. until 18 (19–20–21–22) sts. on right-hand needles, turn and leave rem. 40 (42–44–46–48) sts. on holder.
Next Row	Cast off 4, patt, to end.
Next Row	Cast off 5 (6–6–6–7) sts. patt. to end.
Next Row	Cast off 4, patt. to end. Cast off remaining 5 (6–6–6–7) sts. Return to sts. on holder; with right side facing cast off 16 (17–18–19–20) patt. to end.
Next Row	Cast off 6, patt. to end.
Next Row	Cast off 4, patt. to end.
Next Row	Cast off 5 (6–6–6–7), patt. to end.
Next Row	Cast off 4, patt. to end.
Next Row	Cast off rem. 5 (5–6–7–7) sts.

SLEEVES

With No. 11 needles cast on 49 (52–55–58–61) sts. and work in k. 1, p. 1 rib for 3 ins., fin. with a wrong side row.

Change to No. 9 needles and comm. patt.

Inc. 1 st. at each end of next and every foll. 6th row until there are 91 (94–97–100–103) sts.

Cont. straight until sleeve seam measures 17 (17½–18–18½–19) ins. from beg. (or required length) fin. with a wrong side row.

Shape Top Cast off 3 sts. at beg. of next 2 rows.
Dec. 1 st. at each end of next and every alt. row until 55
(56–57–58–59) sts. rem.
Cast off 2 sts. at beg. of next 14 rows, then 4 sts. at beg. of
4 rows. Cast off rem. 11 (12–13–14–15) sts.

FRONT BAND

Mark position of buttons on suede front as follows:
1st pin 1 inch from lower edge, 2nd pin level with beginning
of front shaping, then two more pins at equal distances
between these two.
With No. 11 needles cast on 16 sts. and work in k. 1, p. 1.
rib for 1 inch, fin. with a wrong side row.

Next Row   k. 1, p. 1 over 6 sts., cast off 4.
Next Row   Cast off 4 rib 6.
Continue in pattern making three more buttonholes at pin
positions, then continue straight until band measures 50
(51½–53–54½–56) inches.
Cast off in rib.

16. A Grain Leather Trouser Suit

Fit the pattern and make any adjustments, taking special note of the join on the trouser legs. This join should always be below the knee-cap and can be either in the form of a straight seam or a 'V' seam. The latter is, in my opinion, the more attractive.

Check that all pieces of the garment have been accounted for in the cutting layout, and then place the pattern pieces on the skin and mark accordingly. Cut and prepare for fitting, utilizing the cellulose tape method.

JACKET

Fit and check, making any necessary slight alterations. Mark the buttonholes and pockets, remove the garment and dismantle prior to cutting the lining and interfacings. Cut the lining as the garment, baste together darts, and then machine and press flat. Join together centre back seam. Iron Moyceel on to facing, trim canvas away $\frac{1}{2}$ inch and pound outside edge.

Nip in leather facing at break of rever (first buttonhole), and glue facing over the edge of the interfacing, working up from the break to the lapel. Turn in rever step to point where the collar finishes on the facing. Secure to the front edge of the lining with paper clips and machine together. Press, allowing the seam to lay towards the back. Join together shoulder seams and side seams, pressing seams towards the back. Iron the Moyceel on to the collar and trim away canvas $\frac{1}{2}$ inch both ends and on the outside edge of the collar. Turn the collar edge over interfacing, mitre corners, and nip away surplus. Secure with adhesive.

A collar with Moyceel interfacings and outside edges secured with adhesive

Coat facings with Moyceel interfacing

Secure the collar to the back neck of the lining, starting at the centre back neck and working towards the front edge of the facing.

Machine the sleeve seams. If bound cuff buttonholes are required these should be done before the sleeve is joined together. Glue the seams open, turn up the sleeve hem and secure with adhesive, leaving the sleeve on the wrong side. Machine sleeve lining and attach to sleeves as directed in previous instructions.

Turn the sleeve lining through and fell it to the sleeve hem, making sure that the lining finishes at least one inch above the fold of the sleeve bottom.

Turn the sleeve on to the right side and press, using a sleeve board or a roller towel.

Top press lining, then place on a hanger until required.

CUFFS

These can be introduced either as a decoration or as a means of lengthening if a shortage of skin is experienced. There are many different types but cuffs are usually divided into two main styles: the full cuff type and the half cuff type, as shown in Figure 24 and Figure 25.

Continue the main part of the jacket, marking buttonholes and pockets, and construct pockets and buttonholes if required. Machine darts, glue open and press. Turn the forepart front edges over and secure with glue, working from top buttonhole to hem.

Join together the shoulders, side seams and glue open. Press. Turn up hem and secure.

Machine under collar on to garment, commencing at the centre back neck and working towards the front of the facing. Reduce excess thickness on the seam ends and glue seams open. Press the jacket.

To attach the lining and coat together proceed as follows:

1: Glue the top collar on to the under collar, making sure that the shoulder seams meet on the lining and jacket.
2: Continue gluing facing to front edge of the jacket, checking the break of the lapel.
3: Catch the lining to the garment at shoulders and side seams on the wrong sides.
4: Top stitch edge of jacket, trimming away skin where necessary.
5: Tack in sleeves, easing fullness at sleeve head and distributing it evenly. Machine sleeve to armhole, trimming away any excessive thickness.
6: Attach lining at armhole and fell lining over armhole edge. Check that the

FULL CUFF TYPES OF POCKETS   HALF CUFF TYPES OF POCKETS

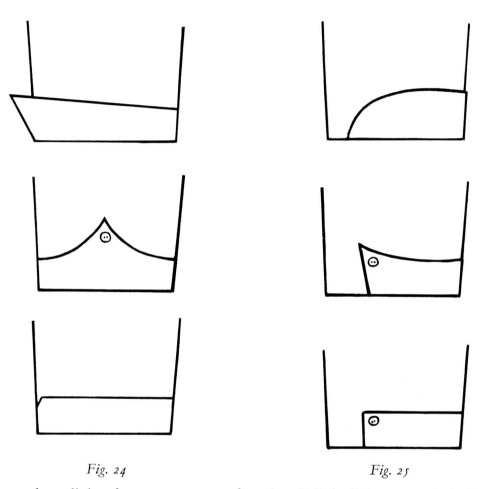

Fig. 24   *Fig. 25*

sleeve lining does not cause any dragging. Fell the lining on to the jacket hem and attach a hanger at the neck.

Press the garment in the usual way.

TROUSERS

When making trousers always allow an extra two inches in length. I have found through experience that suede and leather trousers 'take up' in use; that is, when the leg is bent the trousers tend to 'ride up' into creases, thereby shortening the trouser length. I cannot stress too strongly the need to allow extra length.

Having cut out the trousers, following the usual precautions, cut through the darts to apex and prepare garment for fitting, using the cellulose tape method.

Fit and make any necessary adjustments, then machine darts. Machine back seam using the linen tape method where the tape is placed over the seam line in the seam allowance. The tape is then caught up into the seam as the back seam is machined, which makes for extra strength. Flatten as you would a plain seam and secure with adhesive.

Nip in seam allowance on curve.

Machine the trouser legs where the necessary joins have to be made.

To machine two pieces of suede or leather together using the 'V' method, cut the top section as per Figure 26 and the bottom section as per Figure 27.

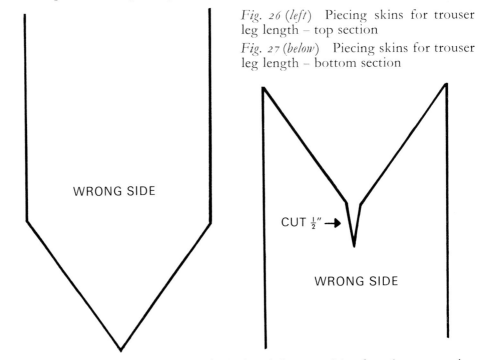

Fig. 26 (left) Piecing skins for trouser leg length – top section

Fig. 27 (below) Piecing skins for trouser leg length – bottom section

WRONG SIDE

CUT $\frac{1}{2}$" →

WRONG SIDE

This section is cut down $\frac{1}{2}$ inch at the 'V' and then machined to the top section as shown in Figure 28.

Press seams open and secure. If edge stitching is required as a decoration it should be done at this stage. Press and hammer away any thickness at the join.

If trouser pockets are required they should be constructed prior to joining the side seams.

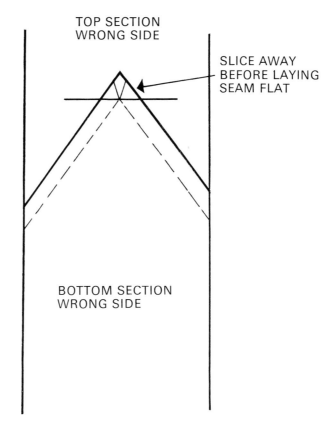

Fig. 28 Piecing skins for trouser leg length – to complete the join

A second fitting could be made at this point. Fly zips are inserted before joining the side seams.

Join together the front of the trousers at the crotch and insert the zip as shown previously. Join the side seams together, press open and secure with adhesive. If a side zip is required, join the centre front of the trousers together and machine the right-side seam as far as the zip allowance. Then insert the zip and machine and secure the left side.

Machine inside legs together, paying special attention to the joins at leg, which should always meet at both outside and inside leg. Press open seam and secure with adhesive. Machine petersham or waistband or trouser top, working buttonhole fastening or stitching on hooks and eyes.

Trouser hems should be secured with a light smear of adhesive. If any length adjustment is required this can then be done with minimum effort and with less chance of spoiling the skin.

Remove handling marks and press.

A lady's two-piece suit in washable suede utilizing six full skins

17. *A Suede Dress and Jacket*

When making a dress it is advisable to use a washable suede, bearing in mind that the simpler the style, the easier it will be to launder the finished garment. The plainness of the style can be relieved by double stitching in various forms.

DRESS

Having chosen the pattern, pin the pattern pieces together and fit, making any adjustments that are necessary. Having done this, lay out the skins and note any flaws, cutting accordingly. Place the pattern pieces on to the skins and mark for cutting, marking right and left sides of the garment. After cutting out the garment prepare for fitting, securing seams with light cellulose tape. Adjust where necessary, using paper clips or pegs to secure the hem.

Dismantle after fitting and prepare to machine. Cut darts through to apex and machine. Stick open the seams using adhesive and press with a medium-heat iron on right and wrong sides. Mark and make the required pockets and buttonholes. Iron on interfacing necessary for collars or facing (this should be a lighter weight than the stiffening used for heavier garments).

Turn over any edges and secure with adhesive. Machine side seams and shoulders, and secure seams.

Insert the zip. Mark the skirt to the desired length and secure with adhesive.

Machine sleeve seam and secure. Fit sleeves into armholes using paper clips, making sure that the fullness of the sleeve head is evenly distributed three inches each side of the shoulder seam and machine.

71

JACKET

Check the skins for flaws, fit and adjust pattern to desired requirements. Cut the lining and suede to adjusted pattern.

From canvas cut top collar and jacket facing, make buttonholes and pockets.

Fit, using paper clips to secure shoulders and side seams. Machine shoulder and side seams, mark the hem and secure with adhesive.

Tack the collar to the neck edge, machine front centre back neck to front and stick open. Cut the lining as garment except for foreparts where facing is joined to the front edges of the lining. Machine the side seams and shoulder seams, pressing towards the back. Machine the top collar starting at the centre back neck.

Stick open seams as in Figure 29.

SEAMS SECURED
WITH GLUE

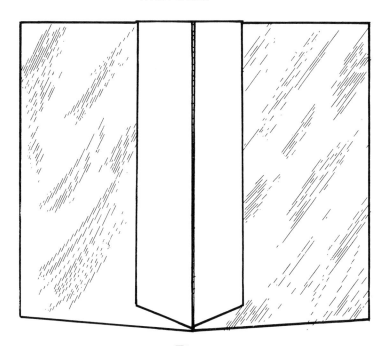

Fig. 29

A suede/worsted three-piece jacket and trousers with matching waistcoat. The jacket takes five skins, the waistcoat two skins and the trousers $2\frac{1}{2}$ yards of 54 inch fabric. Surplus fabric has been used to edge the waistcoat and cover the buttons

Smooth lining with an iron and attach the lining to the jacket by sticking under collar and top collar together at centre back, neck seam to neck seam.

Stick the facings to the foreparts in the same manner.

Machine the sleeves. Stick open seams, fit and mark to required sleeve length, turn up the sleeve hem and secure with adhesive. Machine sleeve lining and press seams open.

Place the wrong side of the sleeve and the wrong side of the lining together, laying seams flat on top of each other.

Commence tacking 2 inches from the top sleeve seam and finishing 2 inches from the sleeve hem. Pull the sleeve lining through and hem the lining to the sleeve.

Press lightly, using a sleeve board or a rolled up towel.

Sew on a neck hanger and buttons.

Brush to restore the suede nap and remove any handling marks.

18. A Shearling Jacket

Shearling is the correct name for a sheepskin garment. When buying the pattern for such a garment, allowance must be made for the natural wool lining; it is therefore wise to buy a pattern a little larger than the size of the garment usually worn.

A plain style is the most suitable, as this can be adjusted or altered to make joins in the most suitable position for the size of the skins. A shearling skin is usually slightly smaller than either a grain or suede leather skin, being an average $5\frac{1}{2}$ square feet.

For a man's jacket with an average chest measurement and of average height, 38 square feet is adequate. If a three-quarter length garment is desired a further 6 square feet are required.

For a woman's jacket with a 36 inch bust measurement an average of 24 square feet will be required, with an additional 5 square feet for a three-quarter length coat.

For our specimen garment in the shearling range I shall detail the making instructions for a single-breasted jacket with welt pockets and set-in sleeves.

This jacket is made with a back yoke and front yokes, this being the most popular type. Having checked the skins for natural faults, either on the suede or on the wool side, pin the pattern together and take the first fitting. Note any alterations that are needed and adjust where necessary. The collar and front yokes are always cut from the same skin to ensure that revers and collar are the same in colour and texture. They should be cut with the shearling lying in the same direction.

Throughout the making of this type of garment all the seams are secured in the same manner, that is with adhesive applied to the seam and then the top seam laid over the bottom seam and hammered flat.

Chalk the pattern on to the skin, making certain of right side and left side of foreparts and right and left sleeves, then cut out the garment.

Prepare for fitting, using either tacks or paper clips to hold the garment together. Fit. Satisfy yourself that no further alterations are necessary, mark pocket positions and buttonhole positions, then unfasten garment.

Take a sharp pair of scissors – hairdressing scissors with long blades are the most suitable – and trim away $\frac{1}{2}$ inch of wool on the following seams.

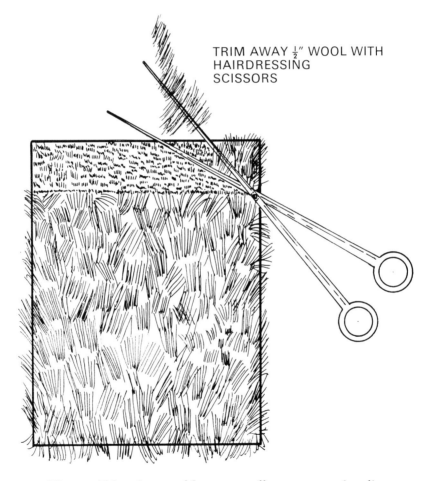

TRIM AWAY $\frac{1}{2}$" WOOL WITH HAIRDRESSING SCISSORS

Fig. 30   Trimming wool from seam allowance on a shearling garment

Deal with the foreparts of the garment first. The yokes are not trimmed at the bottom but the piece of the forepart that is joined to the yoke is trimmed away $\frac{1}{2}$ inch. The same applies to the back yoke. Machine the yokes to the bottom part of the back and foreparts, taking $\frac{1}{4}$ inch seam on the part that has been shaved away (as in Figure 30).

Glue the seam, wrapping the top seam over the bottom seam that has been shaved away, thus ensuring that no ugly seam is visible. Next, shave $\frac{1}{2}$ inch of shearling away on both ends and top edge of the pocket welt. Mitre the corners of the welt, and turn in $\frac{1}{2}$ inch seam on the top edges and the two side ends. Secure with adhesive. Hammer all the corners to minimize the thickness. Machine both ends and top edge of welt $\frac{1}{8}$ inch and $\frac{1}{2}$ inch respectively.

Trim shearling away from the collar, mitring and stitching outside edge and both ends of the collar. Carry out this stitching on the edge of the foreparts, the welt, revers and coat hem.

Cut the binding for the bound buttonholes. This can be either grain leather in a matching shade, or you can use shearling, trimming away the wool from the back.

These pieces should be $2\frac{1}{2}$ inches by $1\frac{1}{2}$ inches, two for each buttonhole.

Now machine revers and edges of foreparts $\frac{1}{8}$ inch and $\frac{1}{2}$ inch in, and mark buttonholes $1\frac{1}{2}$ inches in from the finished edges, as shown in Figure 31.

Shave away the wool from the back of the buttonhole markings. Tack the buttonhole bindings on to the coat, right side to right side, and make the buttonholes as in previous instructions.

Shear away the wool from behind the pocket markings, tack the pocket welt and the pocket bag, and complete the pockets as already shown.

The coat should have a further fitting at this stage.

Assemble the garment, making sure that front and back yokes match at the side seams. Machine together shoulder and side seams, and stick and hammer seams flat.

Trim the wool away from the hem of the garment.

Attach the collar, working from the centre back neck towards revers. Lay the collar over the neck seam as shown in Figure 32, and stitch with straight small hemming stitches, using either waxed buttonhole thread or strong cotton. Trim the wool away from the back seam of the sleeve and machine. Lay the seam flat with adhesive.

Trim away wool from the sleeve hem and machine $\frac{1}{8}$ inch and $\frac{1}{2}$ inch in.

Hammer the hem and sleeve seams to make it easier on the machine. Check the sleeve head in the armhole to see whether it is necessary to adjust the armhole to take the sleeve. (Sleeve head fullness is still desirable even in a sheepskin coat but of course it must be less than in a normal cloth garment.)

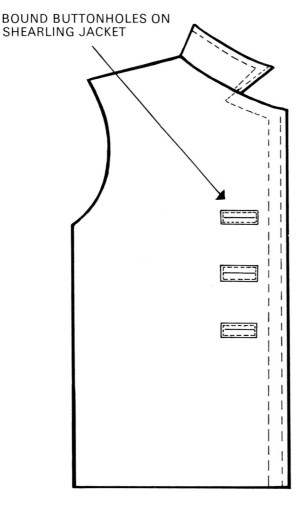

BOUND BUTTONHOLES ON
SHEARLING JACKET

Fig. 31 Bound button-
holes on a shearling
garment

Tack the sleeve in the armhole. Make sure the centre of the sleeve head matches the shoulder seams, fullness being adjusted from 3 inches on back and front of sleeve head.

If the wool is thick it is advisable to trim it away on the armhole sleeve edge. Always remember that the sleeve and armhole should be of equal thickness as one has to support the other. Machine in the sleeve.

Stick the seam, laying it over in the lapping method as shown in Figure 33.

Stitch the buttons on to the coat, using a small backing button, and work a $\frac{1}{4}$ inch neck to allow for the thickness of the wool when fastening the buttons.

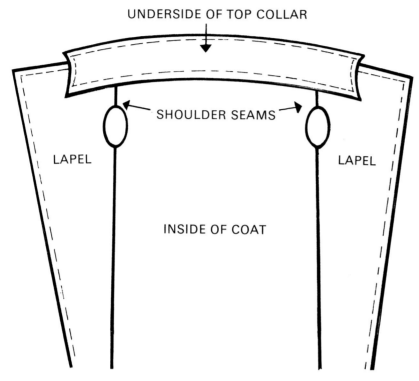

Fig. 32   Attaching a collar to a shearling garment

Place a chain hanger on the back of the collar, using rivets or small backing buttons to secure.

Remove chalk or handling marks, brush the nap to restore suede surface, and the garment is complete.

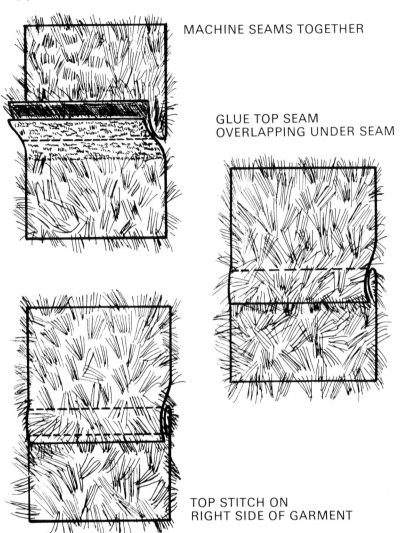

MACHINE SEAMS TOGETHER

GLUE TOP SEAM
OVERLAPPING UNDER SEAM

TOP STITCH ON
RIGHT SIDE OF GARMENT

Fig. 33 Method of overlapping a seam on a shearling garment

19. Using Spare Pieces

APPLIQUÉS

One of the great advantages of working with suede and leather is that all spare pieces can be utilized for one purpose or another. Appliqué work is an example. Flowers, abstracts and figures can be cut out, placed in position with a small dab of adhesive and then stitched to the garment using straight stitching or, with a more modern machine, utilizing zigzag stitch. Contrasting cotton can be used to give a two-colour effect.

FRINGEING

Fringeing is very effective on leather. You must first decide on the length of the finished fringe. This can first be added to the length of the finished garment and then cut, or a piece of leather can be cut to the length of the fringe, plus $\frac{1}{2}$ inch. This $\frac{1}{2}$ inch, used as a seam allowance, is laid on top of the section it is to join and edge-stitched as shown in Figure 34.

BINDING

Binding can be both decorative and fulfil a useful repair job, for example, to a sleeve that has been worn around the cuff edge. This binding can be stitched by hand or machined.

Elbow patches can be cut and stitched in the same manner.

Cut leather binding to the desired length and width plus a $\frac{1}{4}$ inch seam

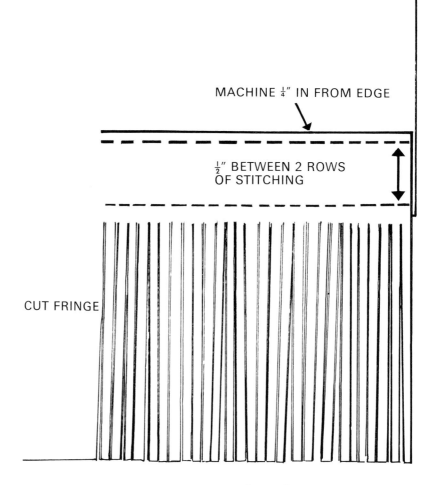

MACHINE ¼″ IN FROM EDGE

½″ BETWEEN 2 ROWS
OF STITCHING

CUT FRINGE

Fig. 34 Fringeing decoration

allowance. Fold the strip in half lengthwise, leaving one side a $\frac{1}{4}$ inch wider than the other. Hammer the edge with a mallet or leather hammer, slip the binding over the raw edge with the wider side underneath and the narrow side on top, and edge-stitch on the top layer. This will then catch the bottom layer.

Another method you can use is to cut a strip to the desired length and twice the width plus $\frac{1}{2}$ inch. Mark a $\frac{1}{4}$ inch seam line along one long edge of the wrong side, fold the strip in half lengthwise, and hammer. Fold in $\frac{1}{4}$ inch seam allowance and hammer, slip the binding over the edge to be bound, and mark along line where the folded edge of the binding falls on the right side of the garment. Match the marked line to the binding seam line, right sides together and stitch the seam line. Turn the binding over the raw edge and stitch into place. Stitch closely to binding edge on the right side using Slipper Foot which will guide the bottom layer.

THONGING AND LACING

Different widths and thicknesses of thongs are available for every type of leather work. Mark out your spacing for the holes with a ruler, about every $\frac{3}{4}$ inch. If on a corner, make a double stitch. This covers the corner which is thereby made stronger. Work with the edge towards you and always thong from the right side of the leather to the back.

Thonging needles may be purchased.

Never use a thong that is too large for the holes. Allow $2\frac{1}{4}$ times as much thong as the length of the edge side of the garment. It is very often necessary to make a join. To do this, shave the end of the thong in use, take another length the same width and shave the opposite edge. Using adhesive, glue both ends sparingly. Place them one on top of the other and form a splice, one shaved on the right side of the leather and one on the wrong side. Hammer gently together, allow to dry and continue thonging.

This type of join may also be used for joining facings and belt lengths.

FROGS AND TOGGLES

These can be bought or made. Unfortunately, the types which are readily purchasable are not usually in the colours required, so it is useful to be able to make them yourself.

Make the frogs by drawing a paper shape and pinning to card, sewing in place by hand where the card overlaps. Fasten the ends at the underside with glue or stitches. Place the frogs on the garment and secure with adhesive. Sew in position, ensuring that all the raw edges are concealed. Sew on buttons to fasten.

TOGGLE LOOPS

Toggle loops are usually made from rope or braid which is cut twice the desired closure length. Secure the ends with adhesive on to tabs, wrong sides together, and place in position on the garment. Top stitch, stitching across braid near garment edge for additional security and on opposite side.

PRESS STUDS

A variety of shapes, sizes and colours can be bought. Punch a hole large enough for the particular type of stud being used. Place the top part of the stud upside-down in the round discs provided for the insertion of press studs, and fit the base of the stud into the hole. Hammer firmly with the part of the tool that has a projection on the end. Punch a similar hole for the end part, put the base of the lower half through the back, place the other part of the stud on top and hammer with the tool (the one with the hollow end). The studs should now be firmly fixed.

EYELETS

Punch a hole in the leather, place the eyelet through the hole and hammer it closed on the wrong side with the appropriate tool. Eyelets can be purchased in various colours and sizes.

PATCHWORK

Odd pieces of suede and leather can be used for making patchwork garments, accessories, etc. Scraps are pieced together after the style of the old patchwork quilts and can be either machined together on a foundation or glued in position and secured with machining.

You can cut flower shapes by making a hole in the centre and threading through a stem with a knot or bead at the end. Leaves may be cut in the same manner and this type of motif can look extremely attractive on a patchwork garment.

Two skins of washable suede have been used for these eye-catching shorts with waistband and decorative pockets. The sides have an artificial fastening using brass eyelet holes and white cord

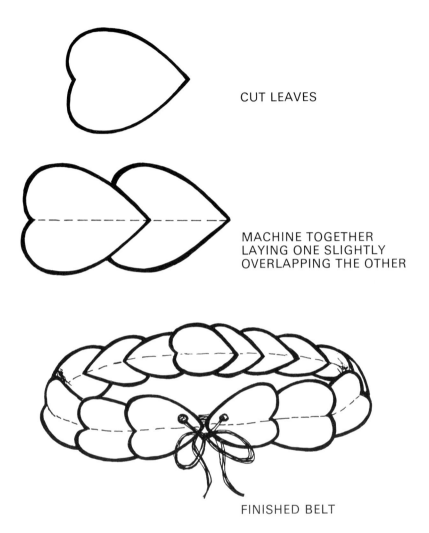

CUT LEAVES

MACHINE TOGETHER
LAYING ONE SLIGHTLY
OVERLAPPING THE OTHER

FINISHED BELT

Fig. 35a   A belt made from leaf shapes cut from leather

BELTS

Belts can be made in the traditional method with stiffening between the belt and the lining, which is usually made in skiver. Eyelet holes can be used as a fastening, together with decorative buckles.

The more modern types of belt can be made of small pieces of suede cut in the shape of leaves or abstracts as shown in Figures 35a and 35b.

Plaits can also be made using strong strands of $\frac{1}{2}$-inch-width strips of suede or leather.

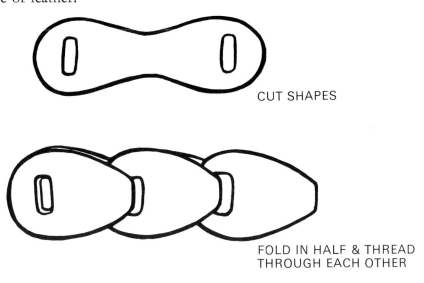

CUT SHAPES

FOLD IN HALF & THREAD
THROUGH EACH OTHER

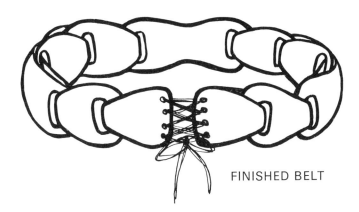

FINISHED BELT

Fig. 35b   A belt made from cut leather shapes, folded and slatted through each other

A stylish evening dress and cape in a very supple nappa leather. This garment takes nine skins of leather and 4 yards of lining

20. Care of Suede/Leather Garments

For all types of garment, careful treatment pays dividends. To wear and casually throw to one side instead of hanging neatly on a hanger will result in an ill-fitting, poor-looking garment.

Suede should be treated with special care and should always be kept away from grease, which is very difficult to remove, although light staining can be removed with the use of a soft pencil eraser. For a stubborn stain, grate a small quantity of blackboard chalk on the affected area. Leave on overnight and brush off in the morning.

Leather garments should never be placed in plastic bags for protection, as suede and leather must be allowed free air ventilation.

WASHABLE SUEDE

Always follow the maker's recommended washing instructions, using the specified product.

NAPPA LEATHERS

These can be lightly wiped with a damp cloth to remove light soiling. All heavy staining should be left to the professionals and you should only take your suede or leather garment to the most reputable specialist cleaning agent.

The classic leather jacket with centre back vent, in this instance for a rather tall man, and using six skins of nappa leather

Glossary of Leather and Leatherlike Fabrics

ANTIQUE GRAIN LEATHER

A grain leather with a surface pattern of markings to produce a two-tone effect.

BUCKSKIN

Suede leather from a deer skin.

CABRETTA

A soft leather with a smooth glossy surface on the grain side.

CALF SKIN

The skin of a young bovine animal not exceeding a certain weight; the various forms depend on the processes employed by the tanner.

CHAMOIS

Originally the split skin of a chamois goat, the term is now used to describe wash leather produced by oil tannage from the flesh split of a skin from a small animal, usually sheep or lamb.

CIRÉ

A high gloss woven or knit fabric to which a heat process is applied, producing a leather-like substance.

CROCK

Minute fibres which rub loose from suede leather on to other surfaces.

EMBOSSING

Surface design raised on real leather skins to produce attractive designs OR a heat process by which a leather-like grain can be impressed upon plastic surface fabrics.

GLAZED LEATHER

Grain leather which has been subjected to a polishing process to give a glazed effect, often produced by applying wax.

GRAIN LEATHER

Leather finished on the outer (grain) surface of the animal skin with the hair removed, leaving the skin pores visible.

HIDE

The skin of a fully grown animal.

KNIT BACK

An artificially-produced leather in which a knitted back is treated with a plastic coating.

LAMB

The skin of a young ovine animal used primarily for clothing or gloving leathers.

A man's double-breasted car coat in nappa leather using seven skins

LEATHER

The skin of an animal, which may or may not bear hair or wool, retaining its original structure, treated in order not to decay or putrify. A general term denoting either grain leather or suede leather.

NAPPA

Grain leather produced from the unsplit skin of a sheep, lamb or goat.

PATENT LEATHER

Leather of which one surface is covered with a waterproof film giving a high gloss surface.

POLYURETHANE

A chemical compound applied to the surface of genuine leathers or synthetics to produce a tough, serviceable texture.

SKIN

A term generally applied to the outer covering of an animal.

SPLIT

Leather which has been divided over its whole area into several layers.

SUEDE

Velvet nap surface produced on leather by an abrasive action.

SUEDE SHEARLINGS

Tanned and finished sheepskin, suede on the flesh (or under) side, the outer surface of which still bears short wool.

Index